YOUR KNOWLEDGE HAS VALUE

Bibliographic information published by the German National Library:

The German National Library lists this publication in the National Bibliography; detailed bibliographic data are available on the Internet at http://dnb.dnb.de .

Imprint:

Copyright © 2018 GRIN Verlag
Print and binding: Books on Demand GmbH, Norderstedt Germany
ISBN: 9783346106094

This book at GRIN:

https://www.grin.com/document/513848

Novi Kesumaningtyas

User Interface Design and Usability. Heuristic Evaluation for Monash's Library Site

GRIN Verlag

GRIN - Your knowledge has value

Since its foundation in 1998, GRIN has specialized in publishing academic texts by students, college teachers and other academics as e-book and printed book. The website www.grin.com is an ideal platform for presenting term papers, final papers, scientific essays, dissertations and specialist books.

Visit us on the internet:

http://www.grin.com/

http://www.facebook.com/grincom

http://www.twitter.com/grin_com

Table of Contents

I. Introduction

Monash Library that located at https://www.monash.edu/library is Monash website for all Monash libraries in all campuses. This website is designed by Monash university not only for Monash students and staff but also for all people who want to access Monash libraries resources. This website provides all services and information that have a connection with access to Monash library's book, data, resource, class, study space, and many more.

Based on the website, the heuristic evaluation had been done and the purpose of this report is to show the Monash library website evaluation based on the Nielsen's 10 Heuristic Evaluation Rules by Jakob Nielsen.

Rule #	Nielsen's 10 Heuristics Evaluation Rules
1	Visibility of system status
2	User-friendly language and conventions
3	User control and freedom
4	Consistency and standards
5	Error preventions
6	Memory recognition rather than recall
7	Aesthetic and minimalist design
8	Help users recognize errors
9	Help and documentation
10	Flexibility and efficiency of use

Heuristic evaluation is used to assess the usability of the product interface to know whether it meets the user expectation or not. By doing the evaluation, we might find a way to improve user experience with the website and also enhance the quality of the website itself.

II. Summary Table

#	Problem	Heuristic Rule	Severity Rating	Recommendation
Task 1 - Booking Study Space				
1.1	It is quite hard to find the booking room link in the page	2,8	3	Give different shape like button shape to the link to make it obivous for the user
1.2	I cannot undo my action if I did a mistake with the room and hours selection even after I clicked cancel button provided	1, 3, 4, 9	3	Give undo option or make the cancel button actually cancel the selection
1.3	After I submitted the timeslot and choose 'Return to Caulfield Library Room' all my selection is gone	6	2	Keep the previous selection so user does not need to redo their booking action
1.4	There is lack of details about what is the color in the table means	7,10	2	Give explanation or legend table for each color
1.5	There is no example how to fill the booking table	5	2	Provide example to prevent mistake in selection
Task 2 - Searching For IT Security Books' Availability and Location in Library				
2.1	It is quite hard to find the search link in the page	2,8	3	Give different shape like button shape to the link to make it obvious for the user
2.2	After I chose Go button in search page, my input is gone and I need to retype again	6,7	3	Directly show the search result after input given and Go button clicked
2.3	Go button in search page is cut and unclear	4	2	Make the Go button clearer
2.4	There is no back button to the Monash library homepage after I clicked 'Go' in search page	1, 3	2	Provide home page button or using same header and footer or make the search page as a new tab page
2.5	I need to sign in again to see the borrowing rights in the 'Get It' tab	5	2	Automatically login after user login to my.monash

#	Problem	Heuristic Rule	Severity Rating	Recommendation
Task 3 - Download Multiple Research About Health Issue from Monash Figshare				
3.1	I can't go back to the last position where I found the article after I go to the detail page	6	3	Remember the last position when user clicked the article
3.2	There is no back button to the search result after I clicked a research article	7	2	Provide back button to the search result
3.3	I need to login again to Monash Figshare even after I already login in my.monash	5	2	Automatically login after user login to my.monash
3.4	There is no notification from the page to let me know whether I successfully download the article	1	2	Give the loading bar or notification about the download process
3.5	It's hard to find how to delete dataset that created by mistake at Monash Figshare My data tab	3	2	Provide the option to delete dataset in the same column
Task 4 - Register Session Class About Exam Preparation at Caulfield Library				
4.1	It is quite hard to find the library class booking system link in the page	2,8	3	Give different shape like button shape to the link to make it obvious for the user
4.2	There is no correction if student made some mistake in email address so it causes user unable to receive email confirmation	5	3	Put confirmation for email address and example of student address
4.3	I cannot filter through the search result event	7	2	Provide the filter function so user doesn't need to read through the whole result
4.4	''Return to booking system' button go to the unclear Booking system page that has no help or guidance about how to back again to Library booking event page	1,3	2	Provide back button to previous Library booking event page
4.5	Booking page theme is completely different with the Monash library homepage, showing inconsistency	4	2	Use same header and footer to maintain uniformity

III.Description of Problems and Recommendations

III.1 Task 1 - Booking Study Space

Problem 1: It is quite hard to find the booking room link in the page

#	Problem	Heuristic Rule	Severity Rating	Recommendation
1.1	It is quite hard to find the booking room link in the page	2,8	3	Give different shape like button shape to the link to make it obvious for the user

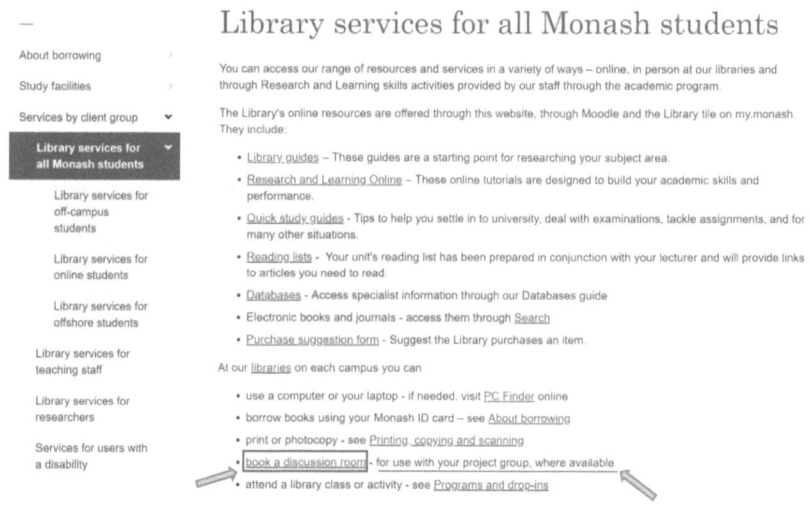

Booking a study space is important for all students yet the way to find the booking way is not easy. To put 'book a discussion room' link as a hyperlink in the paragraph point is somewhat unfamiliar to the user. The user might expect clearer way to book like button shape or bigger navigation. That is why it violated rule 2 where the user somehow unable to relate this hyperlink concept in the real world. The other sentences other than the hyperlinks in the page also fell like unnecessary (e.g., for use with your project group, where available), moreover the other sentences have the same size and font type like the hyperlink. The objective of these sentences seems unclear. It will be better if the library services page only shows the important function instead of hyperlink paragraph so users will have more focus and understand what service that library try to provide to the user. It violated rule 8 where there is unnecessary information that causes a distraction to the main function of the page. The severity rate is 3 based on the analyzing the frequency, impact, and persistence (Hertzum, 2006). I have been booked a study space in the library, and every time I want to book again, I found it hard to remember how to do it and where to find it and not all my friends know that we are able to book a study space through Monash Library web at one glance. Almost all users will find a problem to book the study space through the provided link.

Problem 2: Unable to undo my action if I made a mistake with the room and hours selection even after I clicked cancel button provided

#	Problem	Heuristic Rule	Severity Rating	Recommendation
1.2	I cannot undo my action if I did a mistake with the room and hours selection even after I clicked cancel button provided	1, 3, 4, 9	3	Give undo option or make the cancel button actually cancel the selection

If we made a mistake by selecting the date and the room, and then we hit cancel, it wouldn't cancel the previous selection. Then, if we try to select another available slot before the previous selection gone, there will be a warning that said 'Sorry, the time slots need to be in consecutive order!', while there is no button or guidance to solve that situation. This problem violated rule 1 where there is no indication whether I successfully cancel my selection, rule 3 where there is no option to undo the action, rule 4 where there is different perception about 'Cancel' button meaning in this action, and rule 9 where I cannot find how to solve the problem because there is no help guidance provided. The severity rate is 3 because all user will find the same problem and should be fixed immediately. Suggest adding guidance or when the user hit the cancel button the selection will be gone.

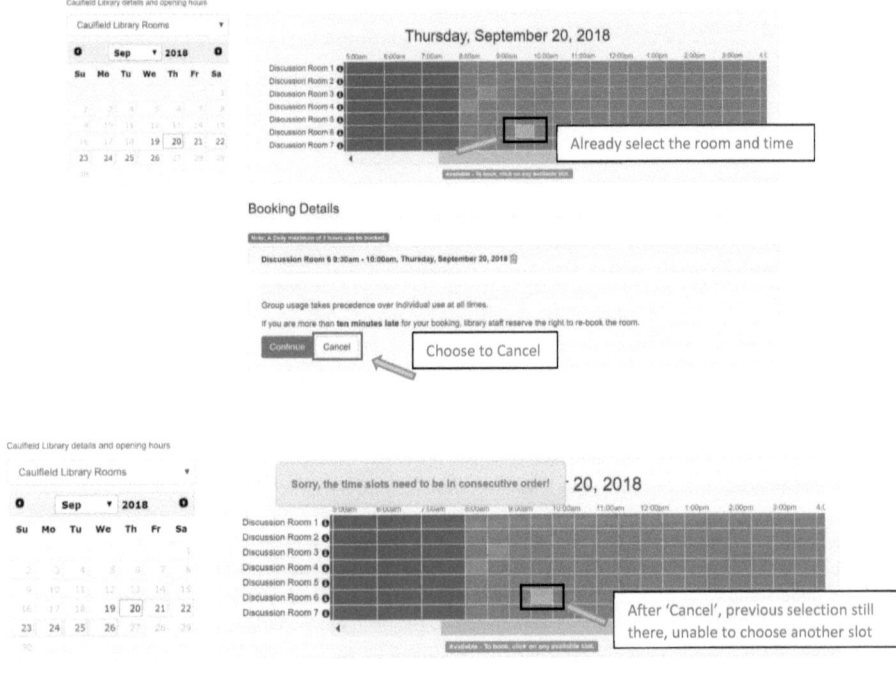

5

Problem 3: After I submitted the timeslot and choose 'Return to Caulfield Library Room' all my selection is gone

#	Problem	Heuristic Rule	Severity Rating	Recommendation
1.3	After I submitted the timeslot and choose 'Return to Caulfield Library Room' all my selection is gone	6	2	Keep the previous selection so user does not need to redo their booking action

I need to select the room and date again if I choose the 'Return to Caulfield Library Rooms' to review my booking selection. This problem violated rule 6 where the user needs to do again in the page that already filled and visited. It will be better if the previous selection still exists or put some warning before the user chooses the button. The severity rate is 2 based on three factors analysis. All users need to spend some time to make the selection again if they hit this button.

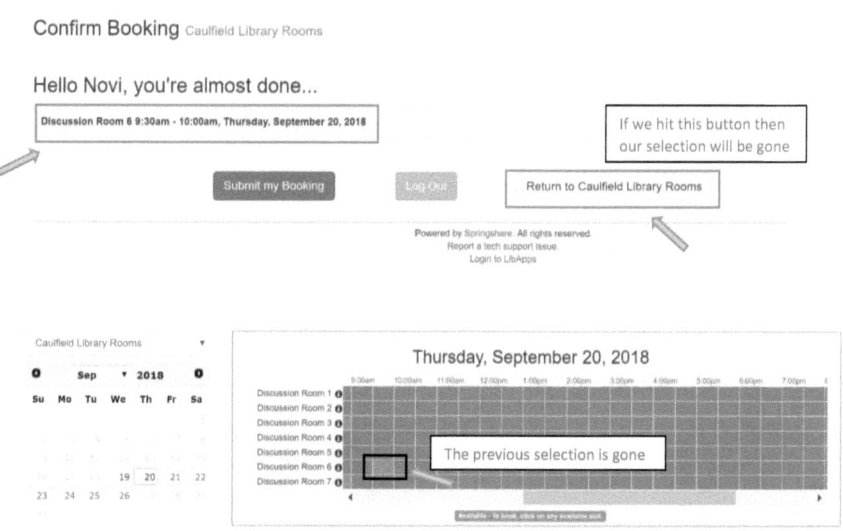

Problem 4: There is a lack of details what is the color in the table means

#	Problem	Heuristic Rule	Severity Rating	Recommendation
1.4	There is lack of details about what is the color in the table means	7,10	2	Give explanation or legend table for each color

The booking page does not provide the legend or guidance what is the meaning of each color in the table except the green one. This problem violated rule number 7 where for the novice users need to guess what each color means before they finally understand through trial and error and rule 10 where there is no help to know the meaning of the color. Suggest providing a legend that explains each color meaning. The severity level is 2. All user needs to take some time or try by itself to catch the meaning of each color.

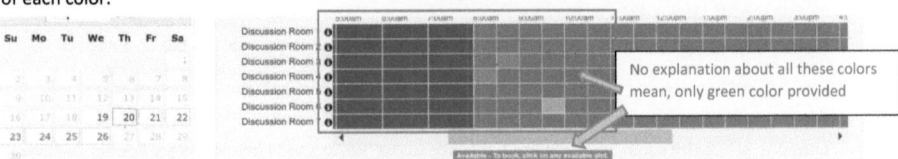

Problem 5: There is no example how to fill the booking table

#	Problem	Heuristic Rule	Severity Rating	Recommendation
1.5	There is no example how to fill the booking table	5	2	Provide example to prevent mistake in selection

The instruction to book the study room is not comprehended with the action we should do on the page. There is a box inside the table that we should select, and the instruction does not mention about the table and what is the box inside the table. There is also no example to prevent user makes a mistake while selecting the box inside the table. This problem violated rule number 5 about error prevention. Suggest providing the example of select the table. The severity rate is 2 based on 3 factors analysis.

Caulfield Library Rooms

Monash students can book a group Discussion Room online to work on a team assessment task, project, presentation or report. Rooms of different capacity can be booked for groups of between 3 to 6 students across the library. Facilities, resources and services are provided at the library branches for the learning and research activities of students enrolled at Monash University.

Failure to use a booked Discussion Room more than 10 minutes after the booked start time will result in the room being available for others to book.

Non-Monash users are free to use other study spaces throughout the library. For further information about room bookings, contact the library.

To make a booking:
1. Select the room, date and time required.
2. Bookings are made in 30 minute slots and for a maximum of two hours per day.
3. Login using your **Monash email address (as username)** and password to submit your booking.
4. Confirmation email will be sent to your Monash email address.

To cancel a booking:
1. Within your emails, search for an email coming from alerts@libcal.com.
2. Locate the cancel link within the booking confirmation email you have received.

If you have other questions, please consult the Information Desk at the library you are making a booking at.

Caulfield Library details and opening hours

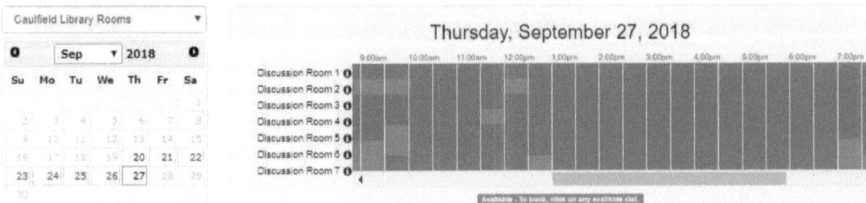

III.2 Task 2 - Searching for IT Security Books' Availability and Location in Library

Problem 1: It is quite hard to find the search link in the page

#	Problem	Heuristic Rule	Severity Rating	Recommendation
2.1	It is quite hard to find the search link in the page	2,8	3	Give different shape like button shape to the link to make it obvious for the user

It is not easy to know how to search article or journal through the Melbourne library. The search is in the hyperlink shape and is located at the bottom of the page together inside a paragraph. This problem violated rule 2 where user somehow unable to relate this hyperlink concept in the real world and rule 8 where there is unnecessary information that causes a distraction to the search function in the page. The severity rate is 3 based on the analyzing the 3 factors (Hertzum, 2006). Suggest giving a different shape like button or magnifier or bigger size to make it clearer for the user.

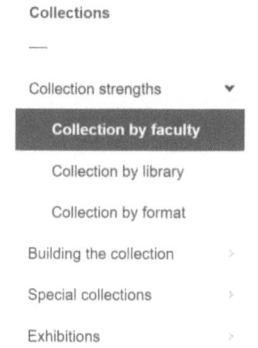

Collections

—

Collection strengths ˅

Collection by faculty

Collection by library

Collection by format

Building the collection ›

Special collections ›

Exhibitions ›

Collection by faculty

Browse the Library's collection by faculty. The Library guides introduce you to the print and electronic resources in a range of subject areas or disciplines.

- Art, design and architecture
- Arts
- Business and economics
- Education
- Engineering
- Information technology
- Law
- Medicine, nursing and health sciences
- Pharmacy
- Science

Use Search to browse the collection by resource type and discover a wealth of material from books, newspapers, journals and multimedia to maps, music scores and images.

Problem 2: After I chose Go button in the search page, my input is gone, and I need to retype again

#	Problem	Heuristic Rule	Severity Rating	Recommendation
2.2	After I chose Go button in search page, my input is gone and I need to retype again	6,7	3	Directly show the search result after input given and Go button clicked

The user needs to do rework when inserting the title of the article or book they want to find because every time the 'Go' button is hit the input will be gone. This problem violated rule 6 where the user should not have to remember information when navigating from one part to another part and rule 7 where it is not efficient for doing the same action two times. It will be better to directly show the result or remove the text box on the first page and let the user do one time on the second page after the 'Go' button is clicked. The severity rate is 2. All users need to realize that they need to do the same action on the second page to achieve the result.

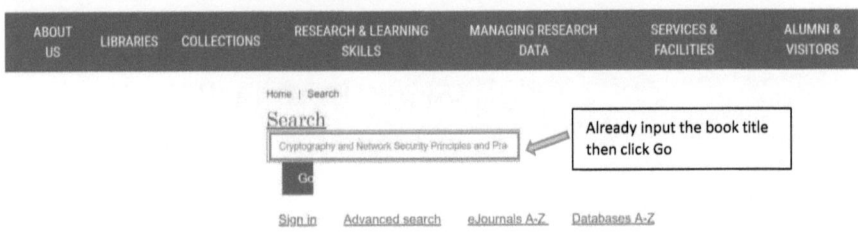

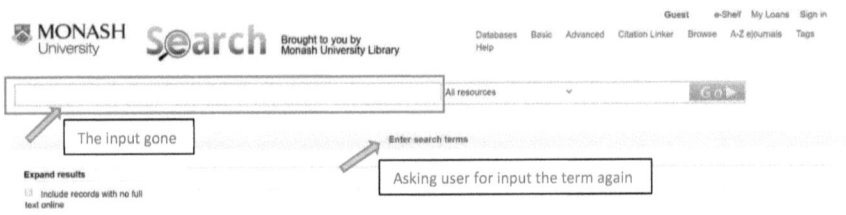

Problem 3: Go button in search page is cut and unclear

#	Problem	Heuristic Rule	Severity Rating	Recommendation
2.3	Go button in search page is cut and unclear	4	2	Make the Go button clearer

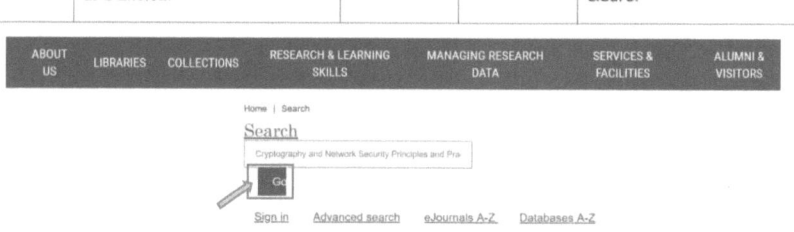

The user is just able to guess what is the meaning of the button below the textbox based on their experience because it is cut and unclear. This problem violated rule 4 where it is not following common standard by showing the unfinished button shape. It will be better if the button gets a fix so it will not confuse the user. The severity rating is 2 since only one button provided so it will not make a big impact for all user.

Problem 4: There is no back button to the Monash library homepage after I clicked 'Go' on the search page

#	Problem	Heuristic Rule	Severity Rating	Recommendation
2.4	There is no back button to the Monash library homepage after I clicked 'Go' in search page	1, 3	2	Provide home page button or using same header and footer or make the search page as a new tab page

After user hit go, the page directly leaves the Monash library page and go to *monash.hosted.exlibrisgroup.com* for the search page. There is no option to back to Monash library page again after user directed to the search page. It is violated rule 1 where the breadcrumbs are not provided and rule 3 where the user cannot exit from this directed page. Suggest to provide a home back button or open the page in the new tab or using the same header and footer with the Monash library. The severity rating is 2 based on three factors analysis.

Problem 5: I need to sign in again to see the borrowing rights in the 'Get It' tab

#	Problem	Heuristic Rule	Severity Rating	Recommendation
2.5	I need to sign in again to see the borrowing rights in the 'Get It' tab	5	2	Automatically login after user login to my.monash

The user needs to sign in again to see the borrowing rights even if the user already signs in for my.monash. This problem violated rule 5 where there is no other way to avoid repetitive action for the sign in. Suggest doing login automatically to every Monash page after student login to my.monash. The severity rating based on three-factor analysis is 2.

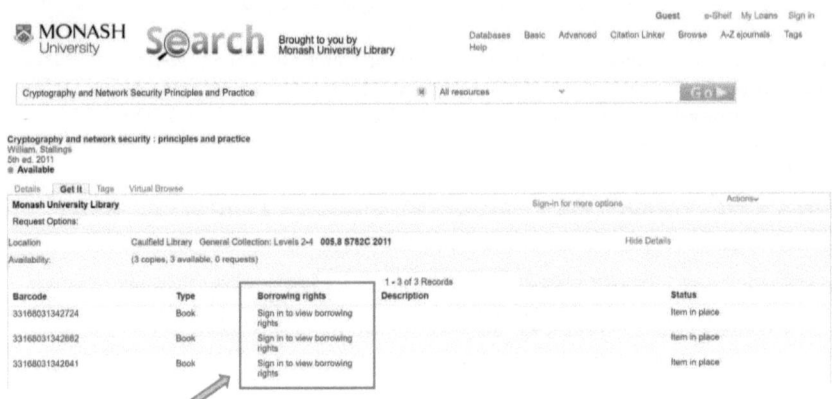

III.3 Task 3 - Download Multiple Researches About Health Issue from Monash Figshare

Problem 1: I cannot go back to the last position where I found the article after I go to the detail page

#	Problem	Heuristic Rule	Severity Rating	Recommendation
3.1	I can't go back to the last position where I found the article after I go to the detail page	6	3	Remember the last position when user clicked the article

After the user selects the research and the page will be direct to the detailed research, there is no option to back to the last position where the user found the article. If the user wants to find another research on the same topic, he needs to search again and going through from the first result again. Moreover, if the user needs to download multiple types of research, this problem will take so much time. It violated rule 6 where the user is unable resuming his exploration in the search result. Suggest to have another open tab or provide the back button that enables to back to the last explore research. The severity rating is 3, it needs to be fixed so research exploration will be more effective for all users.

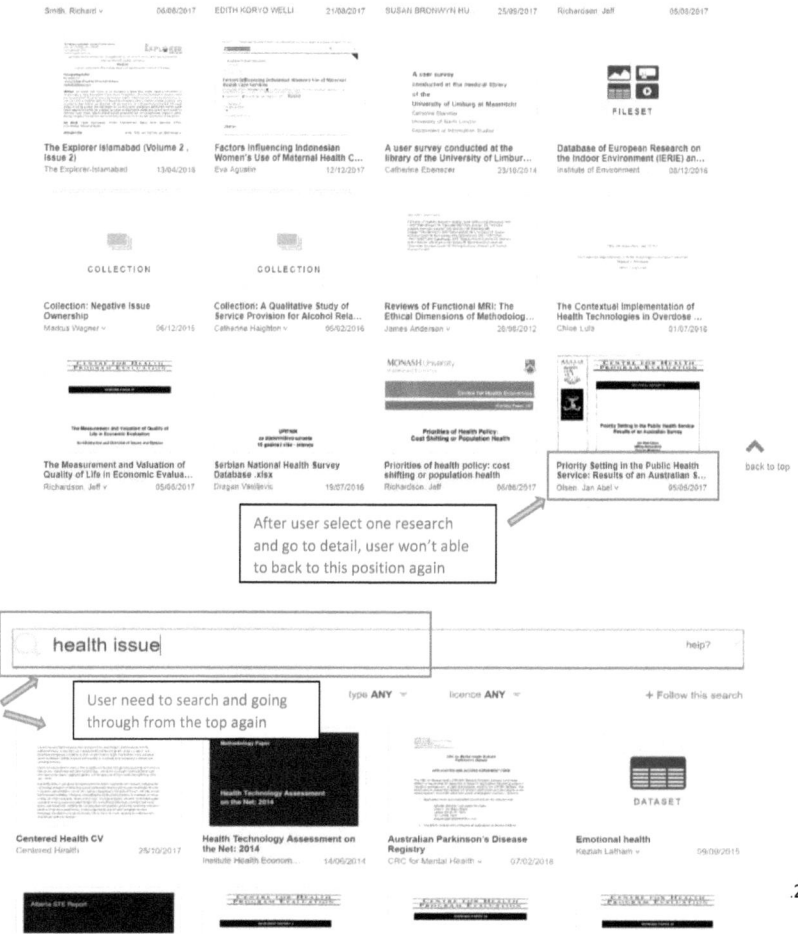

.2

Problem 2: There is no back button to the search result after I clicked a research article

#	Problem	Heuristic Rule	Severity Rating	Recommendation
3.2	There is no back button to the search result after I clicked a research article	7	2	Provide back button to the search result

The user needs to use the browser back button to be able to exit from the research detail page. This problem violated rule 7 where this way is not efficient for each user especially the user that want to download or see multiple types of research. It will be better if there is back to the result button in every research detail page. The severity rating based on three factors analysis is 2.

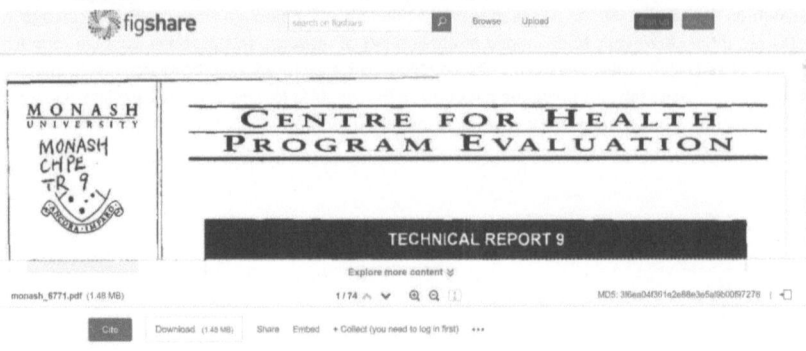

Problem 3: I need to log in again to Monash Figshare even after I already login in my.monash

The user needs to sign in again to use Monash Figshare even if the user already signs in for my.monash. This problem violated rule 5 where there is no other way to avoid repetitive action for the sign in. Suggest doing login automatically to every Monash page after student login to my.monash. The severity rating based on three-factor analysis is 2.

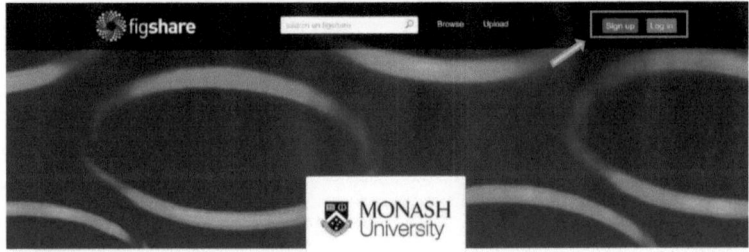

Problem 4: There is no notification from the page to let me know whether I successfully download the article

#	Problem	Heuristic Rule	Severity Rating	Recommendation
3.4	There is no notification from the page to let me know whether I successfully download the article	1	2	Give the loading bar or notification about the download process

The user is unable to know whether they download they successfully download the article or not. This problem violated rule 1 where there is no indication where the task is complete. Suggest having indication or progress bar. The severity rating based on the analysis is 2.

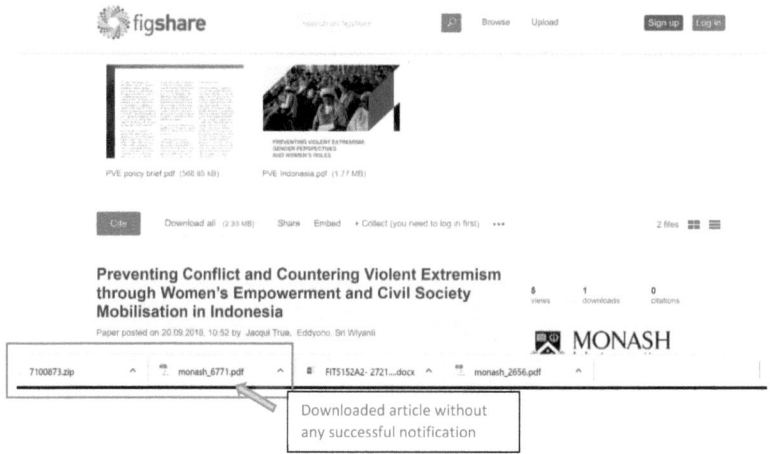

Problem 5: It's hard to find how to delete dataset that created by mistake at Monash Figshare My data tab

#	Problem	Heuristic Rule	Severity Rating	Recommendation
3.5	It's hard to find how to delete dataset that created by mistake at Monash Figshare My data tab	3	2	Provide the option to delete dataset in the same column

User is unable to directly delete the created dataset. This problem violated rule 3 where there is no obvious option to let user undo the action. Suggest providing the option to delete the dataset that located in the same column of the dataset. The severity rating is 2.

III.4 Task 4 - Register Session Class About Exam Preparation at Caulfield Library

Problem 1: It is quite hard to find the library class booking system link in the page

#	Problem	Heuristic Rule	Severity Rating	Recommendation
4.1	It is quite hard to find the library class booking system link in the page	2,8	3	Give different shape like button shape to the link to make it obvious for the user

It is not easy to know how to find a link to booking a session class through Melbourne library. The 'Library class booking system' is in the hyperlink shape and it has the same size and font style with the rest of non-hyperlink sentences inside the paragraph. This problem violated rule 2 where user somehow unable to relate this hyperlink concept in the real world and rule 8 where there is unnecessary information that causes a distraction to the booking function in the page. The severity rate is 3 based on the analyzing the 3 factors (Hertzum, 2006). Suggest giving a different shape like button or bigger size to make it clearer for the user.

Programs and drop-ins

The Library provides education programs for undergraduate and postgraduate students embedded within academic courses in conjunction with academic staff wherever possible. In addition at library branches, further activities are offered that may include the following.

Orientation activities

At Orientation the libraries provide tours, tips on how to get started at university, and training on how to search electronic databases for research. Session information can be found in the

- Orientation planner, or
- Library class booking system (using the name of your home library as a keyword eg "Matheson")

Advice is available

Problem 2: There is no correction if the student made some mistake in an email address so it causes a student to be unable to receive an email confirmation

#	Problem	Heuristic Rule	Severity Rating	Recommendation
4.2	There is no correction if student made some mistake in email address so it causes user unable to receive email confirmation	5	3	Put confirmation for email address and example of student address

If students misspelled their email, there wouldn't be any error prevention to confirm the email address. This will cause the confirmation email never received by the students without student realized. It is because the status in the page is successfully registered. This problem violated rule 5 where there is no error prevention provided when user fill their email detail in the form. Suggest to have example data entry or email input confirmation and show an error if the user put the wrong format. Based on three factors analysis the severity rating is 3 because it might cause students missed the class and it needs to fix.

Unit code:	IT - Keys to Success
Target audience:	IT postgraduate
Presenter:	Dr Andrew Junor
Date:	Tuesday 9 October, 2018
Time:	2:00pm - 3:00pm
Venue:	Caulfield Library Teaching room 3, Level 1, Caulfield
Capacity:	100
Bookings so far:	39
Waitlist bookings:	None
Cost:	Free
Reminder date:	Monday 8 October, 2018

If you would like more information on this event, please contact Andrew Junor at andrew.j

Register

Name:	Novi Kesumaningtyas
Student/Staff ID:	27897176
Phone number:	
Mobile number:	0123456789
Email address:	nkes0001@sudent.monash.edu ← No error prevention for mistake in email field
SMS notification:	☐ I would like to receive SMS notices related to this event. (SMS notices include reminders, cancellations, waitlist changes, etc.)

Register   Return to event listing

- You have been registered for this event

Said registered but I never receive the email confirmation and no notification about email in the page

IT Keys to Success: Exam preparation

Library:	Caulfield Library
Description:	In Week 11, the Keys to Success workshop tackles exam preparation. How should you anticipate exam content and revise for each unit? How can you prepare to write efficient, high-quality exam responses? Join us in Keys to Success, and prepare for a confident exam period.

Please note the content from the Tuesday workshop is repeated in the Wednesday workshop.

Prescribed material:	The Keys to Success workshops use in-class activities and discussion to build your academic skills. The workshops encourage collaboration and interactivity. Please share any of your questions or assignment details relevant to the weekly topic.
Unit code:	IT - Keys to Success
Target audience:	IT postgraduate
Presenter:	Dr Andrew Junor
Date:	Tuesday 9 October, 2018
Time:	2:00pm - 3:00pm
Venue:	Caulfield Library Teaching room 3, Level 1, Caulfield
Capacity:	100
Bookings so far:	39
Waitlist bookings:	None
Cost:	Free
Reminder date:	Monday 8 October, 2018

If you would like more information on this event, please contact Andrew Junor at andrew.junor@monash.edu or telephone 99034410.

Your registration status: Attending

You have successfully registered for this event.

If you are unable to attend, please deregister so that your place can be reallocated.

Name:	Novi Kesumaningtyas
Student/Staff ID:	27897176
Phone number:	
Mobile number:	0123456789
Email address:	nkes0001@sudent.monash.edu
SMS notification:	☐ I would like to receive SMS notices related to this event. (SMS notices include reminders, cancellations, waitlist changes, etc.)

| Update details | Deregister | Return to event listing |

Problem 3: I cannot filter through the search result event

#	Problem	Heuristic Rule	Severity Rating	Recommendation
4.3	I cannot filter through the search result event	7	2	Provide the filter function so user doesn't need to read through the whole result

User need to going through all the search events result without able to do filter action. This problem violated rule 7 where there is no shortcut or search option provided in the page. Suggest having filter function so the user does not need to read through the whole result and check it one by one. The severity rating is from the analysis the three factors 2.

Library class booking system

Search results

Your search for **upcoming** events in the **Caulfield Library** library returned 14 events.

Name	Library	Date	Time	Venue/Campus	Action/status
WARP: Preparing for completion: reviewing, editing and proofreading your thesis	Caulfield Library	Friday 21 September, 2018	2:00pm - 3:30pm	Caulfield Library Teaching room 1, Level 1, Caulfield	Register
Figshare workshop	Caulfield Library	Thursday 27 September, 2018	9:30am - 11:00am	Caulfield Library Teaching room 2, Level 1, Caulfield	Register
IT minor thesis/Honours workshop: Evaluating, discussing and incorporating literature in your writing	Caulfield Library	Monday 1 October, 2018	2:00pm - 3:00pm	Caulfield Library Teaching room 1, Level 1, Caulfield	Register
TDN1002 Workshop: Structure, working with evidence and referencing for your research essay	Caulfield Library	Tuesday 2 October, 2018	2:00pm - 4:00pm	Caulfield Library Teaching room 2, Level 1, Caulfield	Register
TDN1002 Workshop: Structure, working with evidence and referencing for your research essay	Caulfield Library	Thursday 4 October, 2018	2:00pm - 4:00pm	Caulfield Library Teaching room 2, Level 1, Caulfield	Register
IT Keys to Success: Exam preparation	Caulfield Library	Tuesday 9 October, 2018	2:00pm - 3:00pm	Caulfield Library Teaching room 3, Level 1, Caulfield	Register
IT Keys to Success: Exam preparation	Caulfield Library	Wednesday 10 October, 2018	11:00am - 12:00pm	Caulfield Library Teaching room 3, Level 1, Caulfield	Register
IT Keys to Success: Exam preparation	Caulfield Library	Friday 12 October, 2018	2:00pm - 3:00pm	Caulfield Library Teaching room 3, Level 1, Caulfield	Register
BTF590x/BTF1010 Exam preparation workshop	Caulfield Library	Monday 15 October, 2018	10:30am - 11:30am	Caulfield Library Teaching room 2, Level 1, Caulfield	Register
BTF590x/BTF1010 Exam preparation workshop	Caulfield Library	Monday 15 October, 2018	2:00pm - 3:00pm	Caulfield Library Teaching room 2, Level 1, Caulfield	Register
IT minor thesis/Honours workshop: Effective oral presentation	Caulfield Library	Monday 15 October, 2018	2:00pm - 3:00pm	Caulfield Library Teaching room 1, Level 1, Caulfield	Register
BTF590x/BTF1010 Exam preparation workshop	Caulfield Library	Tuesday 16 October, 2018	11:00am - 12:00pm	Caulfield Library Teaching room 2, Level 1, Caulfield	Register
BTF590x/BTF1010 Exam preparation workshop	Caulfield Library	Tuesday 16 October, 2018	1:00pm - 2:00pm	Caulfield Library Teaching room 2, Level 1, Caulfield	Register
WARP: Oral presentation practice session	Caulfield Library	Friday 19 October, 2018	2:00pm - 3:30pm	Caulfield Library Teaching room 3, Level 1, Caulfield	Register

Problem 4: 'Return to booking system' button go to the unclear Booking system page that has no help or guidance about how to back again to Library booking event page

#	Problem	Heuristic Rule	Severity Rating	Recommendation
4.4	'Return to booking system' button go to the unclear Booking system page that has no help or guidance about how to back again to Library booking event page	1,3	2	Provide back button to previous Library booking event page

There is no option to back to Library booking event page again after user directed to Booking system page. It is violated rule 1 where the breadcrumbs are not clear and rule 3 where the user cannot exit from this directed page. Suggest to provide a back button or open the page in the new tab. The severity rating is 2.

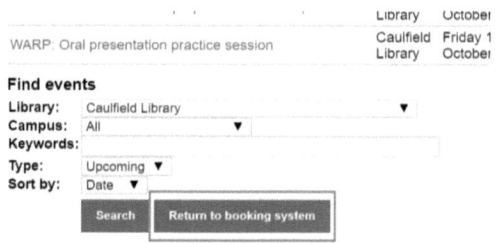

MONASH
University

Booking systems

- Access Monash Mentor Events booking system
- Arts Educational Design Event Booking System
- Arts Global Programs Events Booking System
- Arts Graduate Research booking system
- Arts Online Presence Program team booking system
- Arts Peers Ambassadors Leaders (PAL) Program Booking System
- Arts Student Services Course Advice booking system
- Arts Teaching and Learning Events Booking System
- Better Learning and Teaching (BLT) booking system
- Buildings and Property Division
- Campus Community Division Events Booking
- Centre for Undergraduate Research Initiatives and Excellence (CURIE)
- Chancellor's Installation
- CIO Portfolio booking system
- Diversity and Inclusion Booking System
- Faculty of Arts Research Business and Development Office Booking System
- Faculty of Education booking system
- Faculty of Engineering & Information Technology booking system
- Faculty of IT booking system
- Faculty of Law Booking System
- Faculty of Medicine, Nursing and Health Sciences Booking System
- Faculty of MNHS PhD Training Program booking system
- Faculty of MNHS Research Office Events
- Faculty of Science Booking System
- FIT HDR Student Committee Clayton Booking System
- FMNHS Graduate Research Booking System
- FMNHS HDR Writing and Communication booking system
- GENERATOR Booking System
- Graduate Education seminar booking system
- HDR Central Clinical School booking system
- Health and wellbeing events booking system
- Jobs for students interview
- Library class booking system
- MCEM New Project Meeting Booking System
- MERIT Program Booking System
- Microbiology Department Booking System
- Monash Abroad booking system

Problem 5: Booking page theme is completely different with the Monash library homepage, showing inconsistency

#	Problem	Heuristic Rule	Severity Rating	Recommendation
4.5	Booking page theme is completely different with the Monash library homepage, showing inconsistency	4	2	Use same header and footer to maintain uniformity

Inconsistency in the theme makes the users confused about the page and suddenly become unfamiliar with the page. This problem violated rule 4 where the page does not follow the consistency. Suggest using the same header and footer to keep the uniformity to make the user understand how to operate the booking page fastly. The severity rating based on the three-factor analysis is 2.

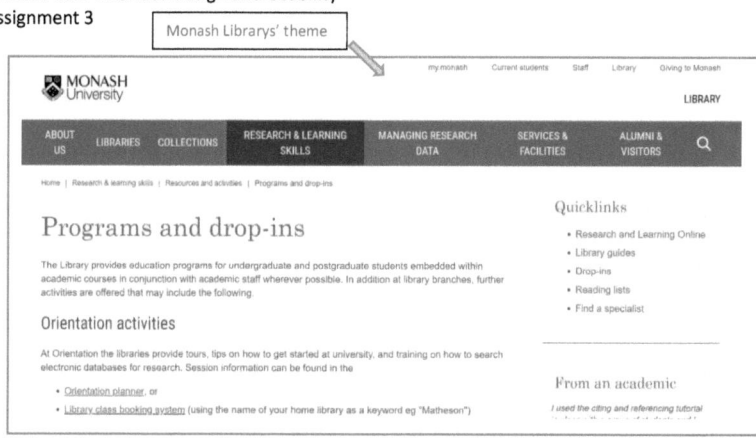

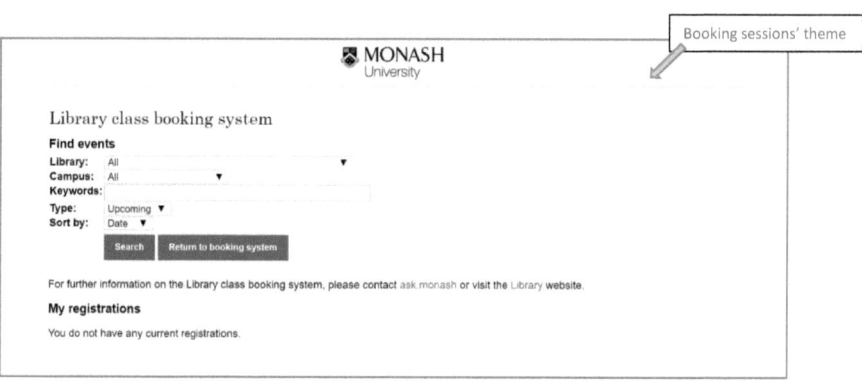

III. Conclusion

Based on the heuristic evaluation we can see there are some problems regarding the user experiences and usability with the websites. These problems severity is ranging from major to minor usability problem which major means that the problems are important to fix. From the reference (Kan Peng, 2004) it says that while experts tend to reveal more serious problems, novices are better evaluator because of they are able to find more problems than the experts. It means that even though the designer of the Monash library website feels that some bug probably only finds by novice user and it is not a big issue, it might be the main reason of some important information unable to deliver to the potential library customer. For example, a novice user will think library website is more to find a book and study place in the library, yet it is not easy to find that functions through the Monash library website. Too many information tries to deliver with some inconsistent design.

This report means to explain 20 problems found from the website library including the suggestion, if some of these suggestions are taken by Monash library, the user usability and experience might be better in the future, and the traffic of the website might be higher.

IV. References

Issa, T., & Isaias, P. (2015). Usability and Human Computer Interaction (HCI). In Sustainable Design (pp. 19-36). Springer, London.

Kan Peng, L., Ramaiah, C. K., & Foo, S. (2004, March). Heuristic-based user interface evaluation at Nanyang Technological University in Singapore. Vol.38, pp.42-59.

Nielsen, J. (1989, September). Usability engineering at a discount. In Proceedings of the third international conference on human-computer interaction on Designing and using human-computer interfaces and knowledge based systems (2nd ed.) (pp. 394-401). Elsevier Science Inc.

Nielsen, J. (1995). 10 usability heuristics for user interface design. Nielsen Norman Group, 1(1).

FIT5152 User Interface Design and Usability
Assignment 3

V. Appendix

- Task 1: HTA for Booking Study Space

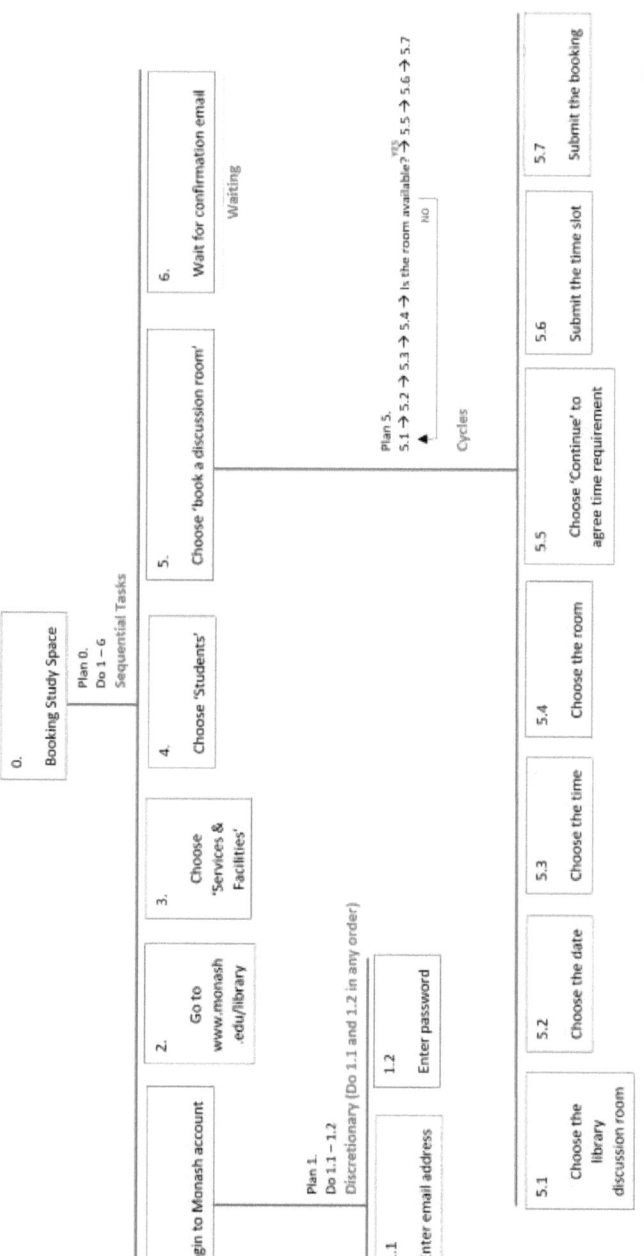

FIT5152 User Interface Design and Usability
Assignment 3

- Task 2: HTA for Searching for IT Security Books' Availability and Location in Library

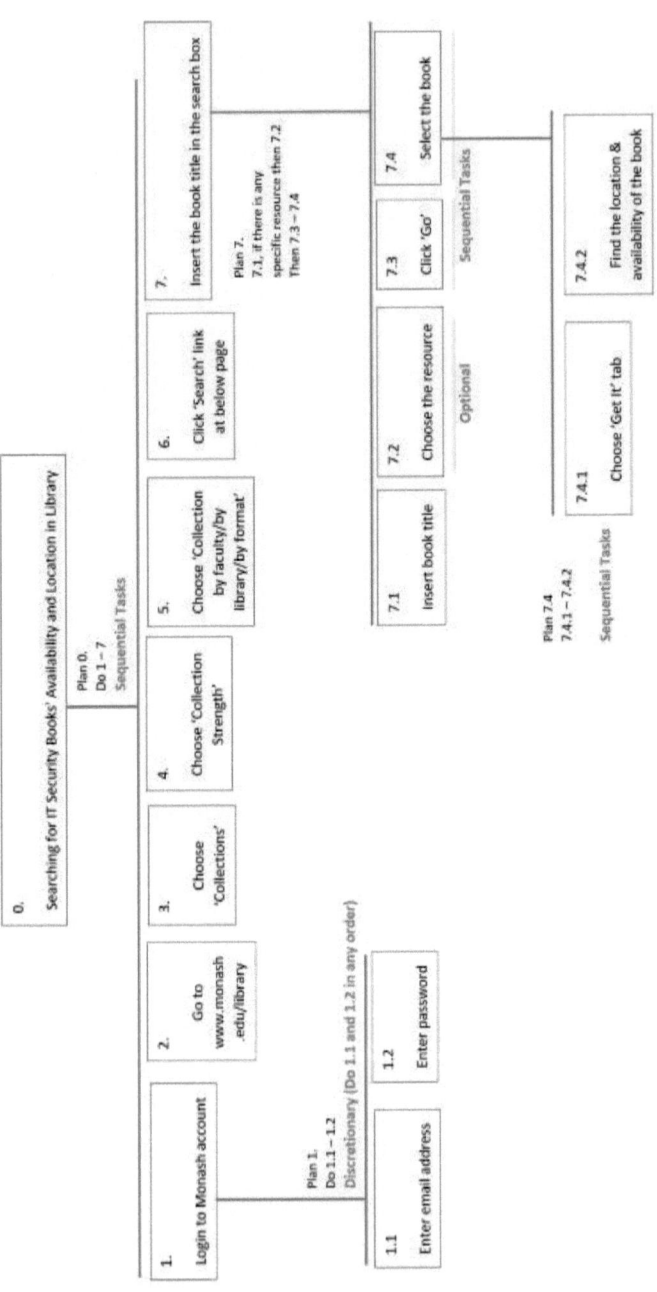

FIT5152 User Interface Design and Usability
Assignment 3

- Task 3: HTA for Download Multiple Research About Health Issue from Monash Figshare

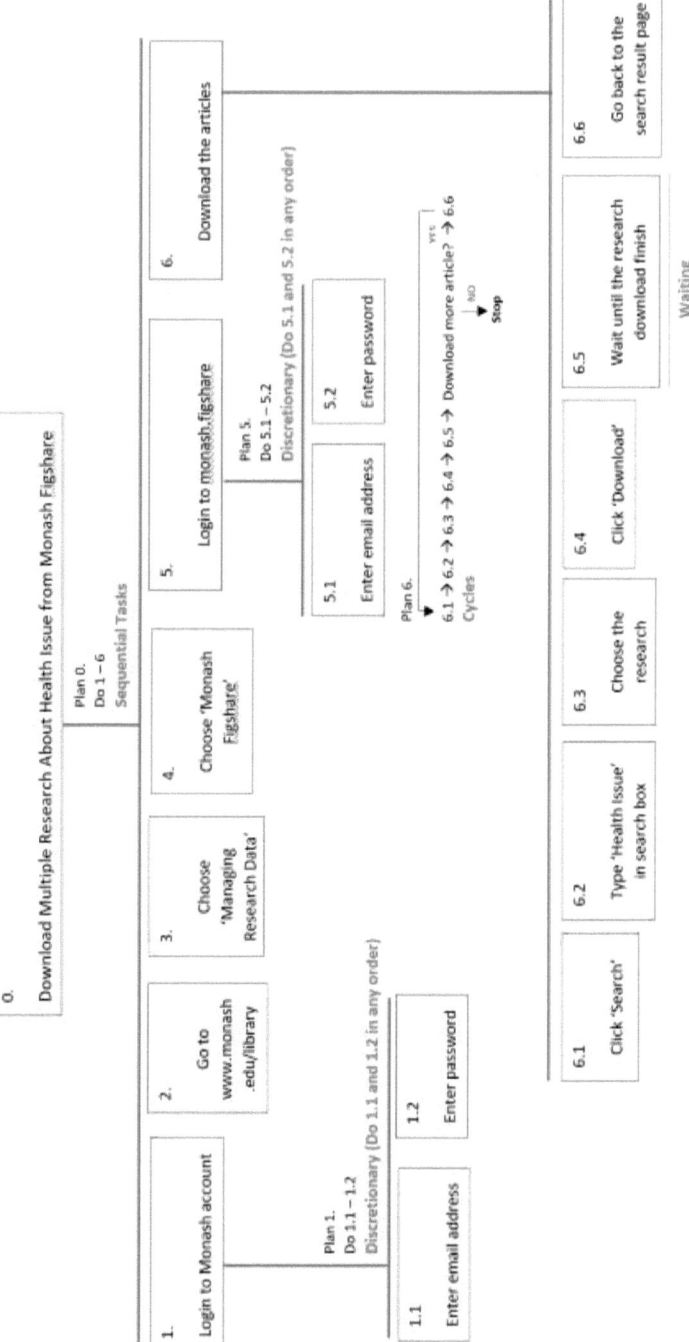

0.
Download Multiple Research About Health Issue from Monash Figshare

Plan 0.
Do 1 – 6
Sequential Tasks

1.
Login to Monash account

Plan 1.
Do 1.1 – 1.2
Discretionary (Do 1.1 and 1.2 in any order)

1.1
Enter email address

1.2
Enter password

2.
Go to www.monash.edu/library

3.
Choose 'Managing Research Data'

4.
Choose 'Monash Figshare'

5.
Login to monash.figshare

Plan 5.
Do 5.1 – 5.2
Discretionary (Do 5.1 and 5.2 in any order)

5.1
Enter email address

5.2
Enter password

6.
Download the articles

Plan 6.
6.1 → 6.2 → 6.3 → 6.4 → 6.5 → Download more article? → 6.6
Cycles

YES

NO
Stop

6.1
Click 'Search'

6.2
Type 'Health Issue' in search box

6.3
Choose the research

6.4
Click 'Download'

6.5
Wait until the research download finish

Waiting

6.6
Go back to the search result page

FIT5152 User Interface Design and Usability
Assignment 3

- Task 4: HTA for Register Session Class About Exam Preparation at Caulfield Library

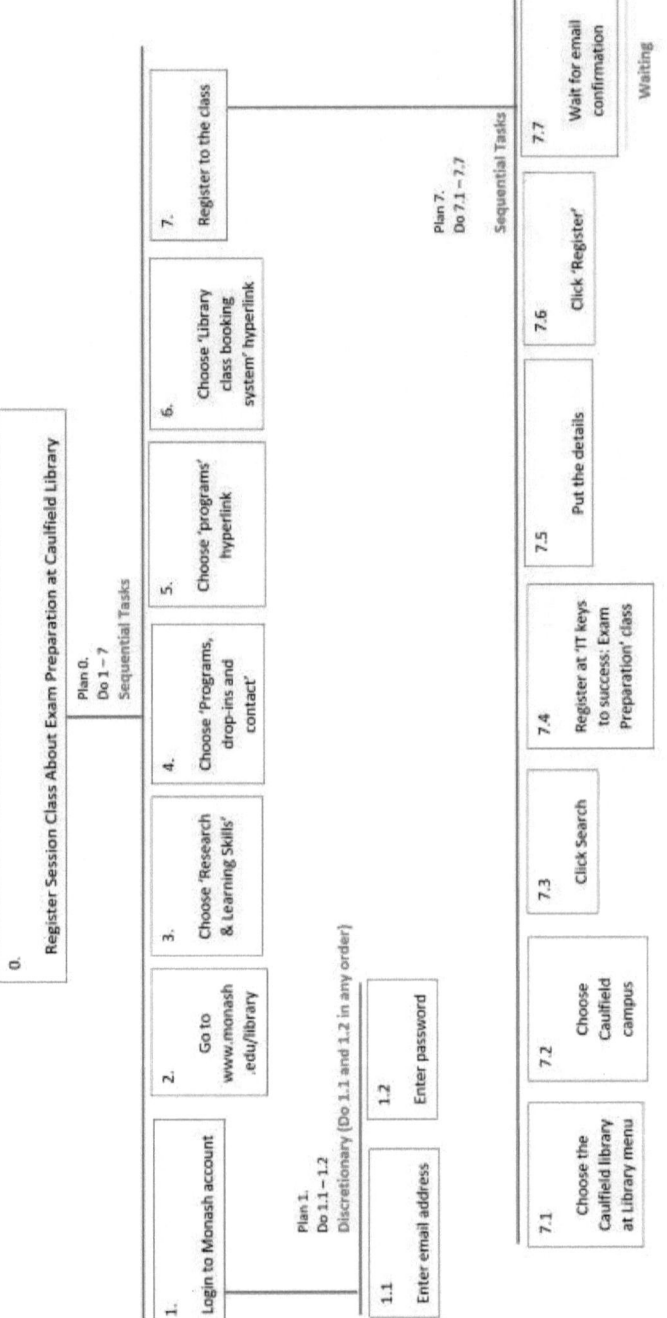